YOU'RE
YOUR
OWN
COMPASS

Believe
In
Your
Vision

Unearth
Untold
Universes

PERSIST
PLUNGE
PROSPER

Thrive Through Tenacity

Dedicate To The Dream

DRIVEN
BY
DESIRE

Embrace
Every
Edge

Generate
Glowing
Gusto

find
Strength
in
Struggles

VISIONARY
VIBES
VALIDATE

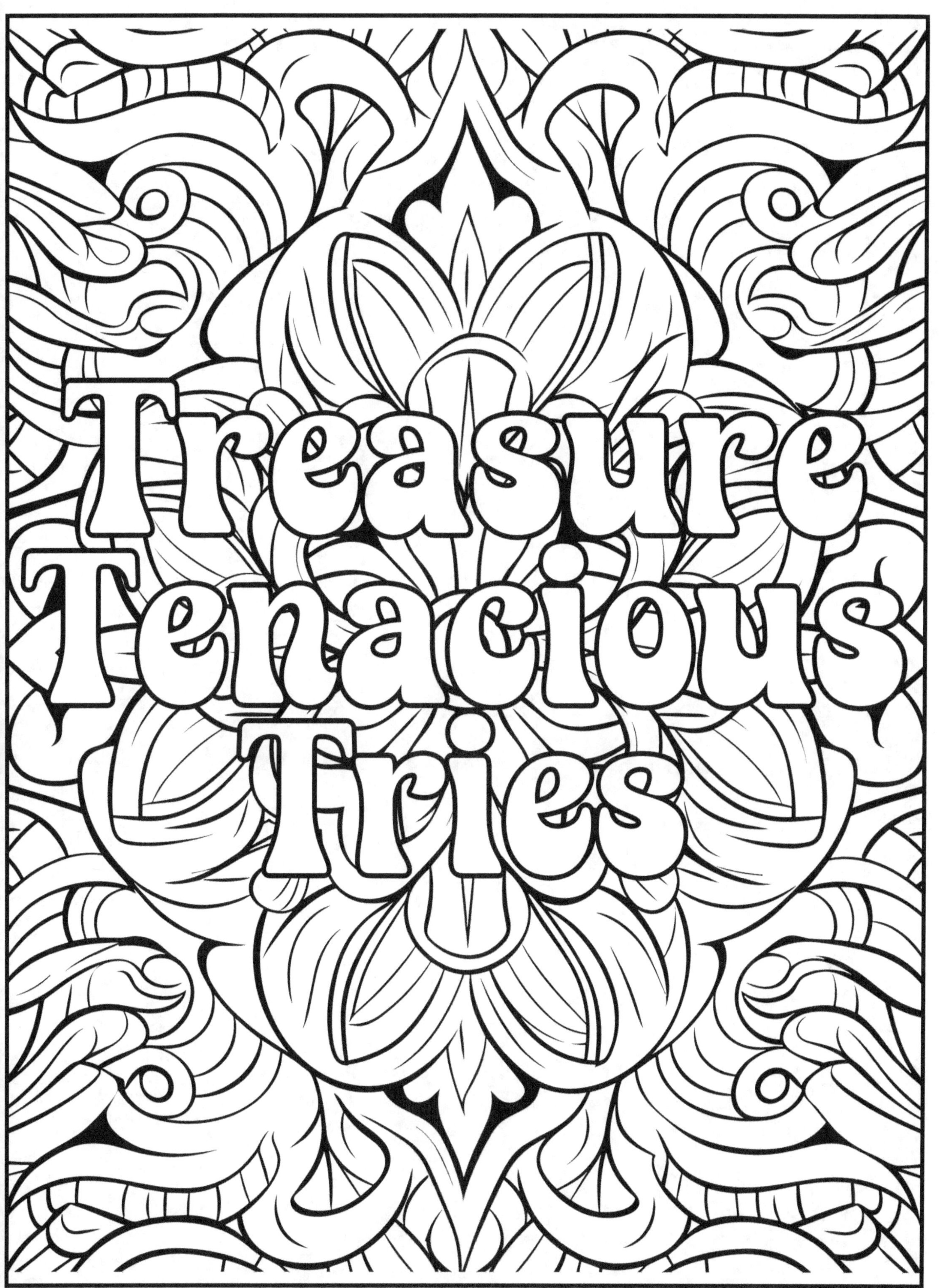

Treasure
Tenacious
Tries

Steer
your
Story

You
Hold
The
Power

Zoom
Beyond
Zones

Tread
The
Trail

Pulse
With
Purpose

JOURNEY
JOYFULLY

Belief
Is
The
Seed

Craft
Not
Chance

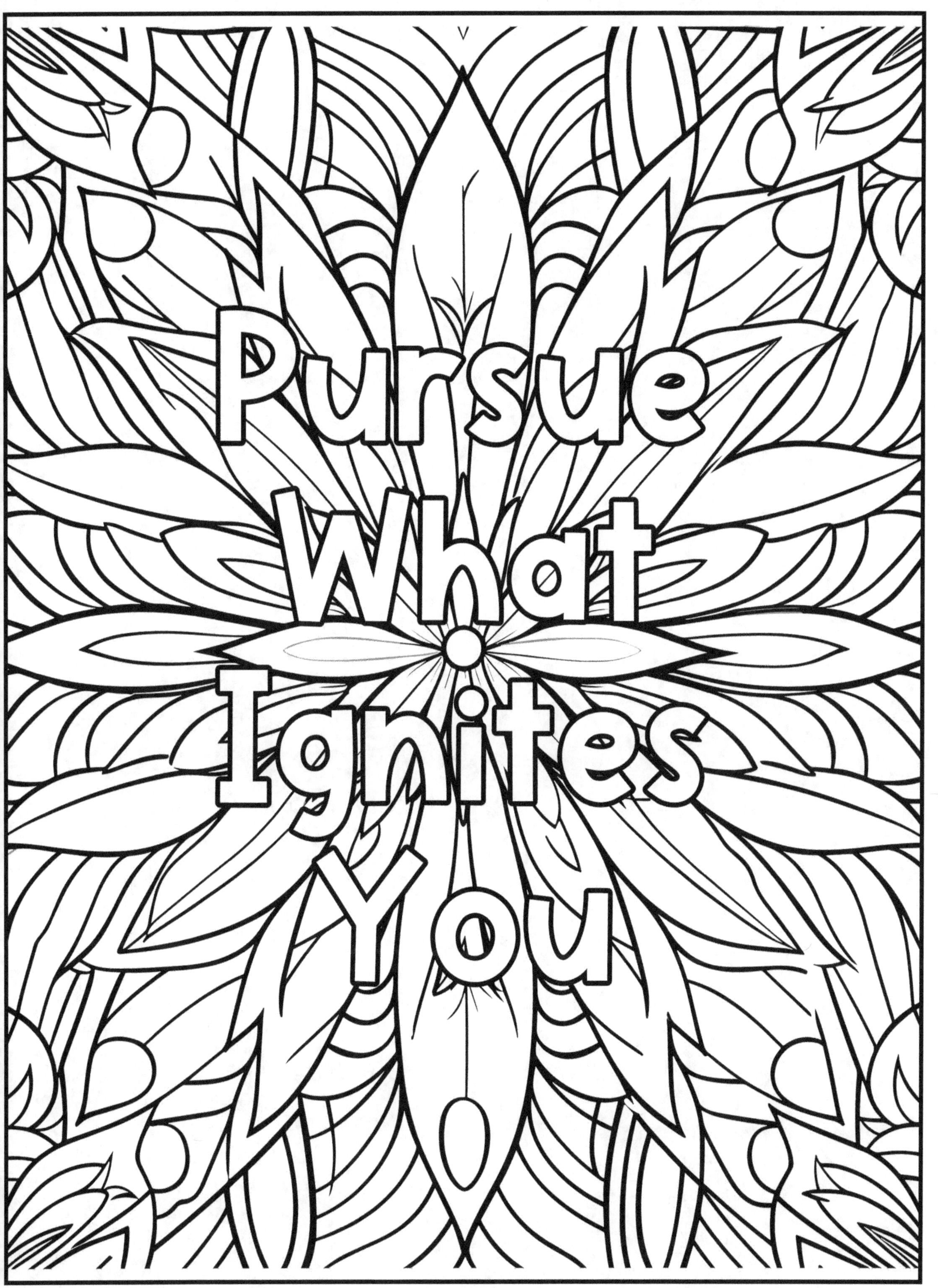

Pursue
What
Ignites
You

HEART
OVER
HURDLES

Hope
Hustle
Harvest

Harbor
Heartfelt
Hopes

Yield
To
Your
Yearning

RECLAIM
RADIANT
REWARDS

Jumpstart
Joyous
Journeys

Liberate
Lofty
Limits

NURTURE
NOBLE
NUANCES

GALVANIZE
AND
GROW

FUEL
YOUR
FIRE
FIERCELY

HARNESS
HOPE

X-MARK
MOMENTS
MATTER

Blossom
Boldly

Ignite
The
Fire
Within

CHAMPION
CHANGE
WITHIN

With
Will
Win

Hold
The
Horizon

CONQUER
FROM
WITHIN

Triumph Through Tenacity

Your
Story
Your
Strength

Always
Aim
Aloft

Jumpstart
Jubilant
Journeys

Growth
Starts
Within